S0-ANQ-362

Positive Reinforcement Activities

Grades 7 - 12

Staff Writer Ellen Stone Doukoullos

Editorial Staff Marlene Canter, Carol Provisor,
Barbara Schadlow, Kathy Winberry

Project Manager Sue Lewis

Design Linda Roden-Gill

Educational Consultants Bert Simmons, Harriett Burt

© 1987 Lee Canter & Associates
P.O. Box 2113, Santa Monica, CA 90407-2113
800-262-4347   310-395-3221

ISBN #0-939007-02-9

Printed in the United States of America
First printing January 1987; Seventh printing August 1992

Contents

Section III

Positive Reinforcement for the Entire School

Introduction

"I shouldn't have to praise my students or give them rewards; they should just be good all the time!"

How many times have we heard this from educators? How many times have you as an educator said it? Yet we know that being "good all the time" is an unrealistic expectation for youngsters as well as for adults. And it ignores the fact that no one, whether teenager or adult, likes to be taken for granted.

When teachers are asked if they feel better about themselves when they are praised, and whether the praise causes them to repeat the behavior which earned the praise, they unhesitatingly answer "yes." When they are asked if they, as individuals or as a profession, receive enough praise, they immediately answer a resounding "no!" Yet those teachers are doing what they are supposed to be doing — "being good all the time."

Praise and Appreciation Are Important Motivators

Good teachers are doing what they are paid to do, and yet they notice and resent as individuals and as a profession the lack of praise, appreciation and respect they receive. In the same way, you may expect students to behave because they are supposed to behave and because good grades, like your paycheck, are thought to be adequate validation and reward.

We know that most students today *aren't* good all the time. When we grew up, adults in authority commanded respect. But times have changed. The breakdown of the traditional family, the deterioration of many of our schools, and the expanded freedom of our young people have had an effect on their behavior in the classroom. Spending all day giving out disciplinary consequences is not the answer to getting through to these students. To see an improvement in their behavior, you need to employ a more positive approach.

Positive Consequences Change Behavior

Every effective school study has shown that the most successful schools accentuate the positive in their disciplinary approach to students. Educators in these schools know that negative consequences *stop* inappropriate behavior and that positive consequences *change* inappropriate behavior. They know that reinforcement of appropriate behavior causes a person to repeat the behavior that earned the praise. How many times have you been praised by your administrator or your spouse for a particular behavior and then found yourself repeating that behavior because you now have a "reputation" for it which you wish to keep? The same principle applies to students.

That's all very well for elementary schools, you might think. But junior high is different. And high school kids just can't handle being singled out for praise and think rewards are dumb. You may believe that positive reinforcement just won't work with secondary kids. Or that students don't want praise because they shrug it off, turn away, or grimace when it is given. The truth is, secondary students love praise, and will respond to it as long as it is given with care.

Adolescents, in particular, have a special need for a positive mirror held up to them because they so often set such high standards and feel they fall so far short. Adolescents are among the neediest of all children for praise, support and validation. Yet, paradoxically, they make it the hardest for the adults in their lives to give it to them. The need to be cool, the need for peer acceptance, the separation struggle from parents and school, and their often low acceptance of themselves make them immediately and overtly resistant to any attempt to reinforce them.

Your challenge as an educator is to overcome the adolescents' roadblocks to acceptance of praise and validation. You must use sensitivity and skill in applying a variety of reinforcement strategies from praise to group incentive systems.

Positive Reinforcement Is Effective with Adolescents

Positive reinforcement can be as simple as a few extra words of praise written on a paper or discreet verbal praise out of earshot of peers. It can be a positive phone call or a post card to parents. (Some parents have never received positive words about their children!) It may be a shared positive experience for the whole class or the entire school, such as a surprise after-school dance.

Keep in mind as you develop your positive reinforcement system that it is often the "superstars" who are singled out for praise. Chronic or severe behavior problems, too, receive positive reinforcement at the hands of skilled disciplinarians who know it is an important tool in redirecting behavior. One group, however, is often left out. These are the very quiet, withdrawn students who go to class on time, bring their materials, don't act out, earn good enough grades to get by, and don't "bother" anybody. Be aware of these "quiet" ones and make a special effort to notice them and "catch them being successful."

The reward incentives you choose to use with students must meet your professional standards, feel comfortable for you to use, and be delivered in a sincere manner. This supplementary book to Lee Canter's *Assertive Discipline Text* gives you specific techniques (and reproducibles) to use for motivating good student behavior. The ideas in this book represent proven methods and materials, used by junior high and high school teachers all over America. These suggestions for positives have been tested in urban, suburban, and rural areas, with average, remedial, and accelerated students of all socio-economic backgrounds.

Have Fun with Positives - and Reap the Benefits

We are well aware that you may be facing 150-200 students in changing classes five to seven times a day. We realize that you yourself may not be teaching in the same classroom all day. Consequently, we acknowledge that using positive reinforcement effectively under these conditions may be one of the hardest challenges you as a secondary educator face.

But the more you recognize students for their good behavior, the less you'll have to deal with their misbehavior. Have fun with your positives, and the atmosphere in the classroom will reflect it with the excitement, cooperation and achievement you've always dreamed of.

Positive Reinforcement for Individual Students

To build well-behaved classes, each individual student needs to experience positive reinforcement. The following proven suggestions are just a few that help students learn that their behavior is noticed all the time, even though rewards are intermittent.

Rewards for Individual Students

- Principal's parking space for a day
- Free pass to school dance or school sporting event
- Disc jockey for an hour on local radio station
- Student-of-the-Week featured in local newspaper
- Song dedicated to a student on local teen music station
- 10 minutes of note-writing to anyone
- 30 minutes with a headset during class study time
- Free Junior Prom ticket
- Free ice cream at lunch
- Teen magazine time at special V.I.P. table in cafeteria (magazines screened)
- Cafeteria Cut Pass: student goes to the head of the line
- Movie pass (donated by merchants)
- Free gift certificates to restaurants (donated)
- Perfect Attendance Award: certificate to the student plus a copy for student's permanent record file
- Positive phone call to parents from teachers, counselors, principal
- School pencils, stickers, T-shirt
- Skip one homework assignment

- Extra computer time
- Lunch with a friend in a special area of the campus that is usually off-limits
- Private praise

Private Praise   Many students in junior high school and high school respond better to praise given privately. It is important not to single out an older student in front of his or her peers. This leads to catcalls and other problems of "favoritism." Praise the student when the two of you have a moment alone, or write your positive comments on an assignment that will be returned to the student.

Positive Post Cards to Parents

Have all students self-address special post cards that you plan to send to their parents with positive comments about the student. It is nice to have cards pre-printed by the school with headlines such as 'Congratulations!" or "Good News!" A few more words jotted by the teacher, administrator, or counselor will brighten the parents' day, and encourage positive parental participation.

Students will look for their post cards in the mail, especially if they are working toward a specific behavior improvement.

Keeping the post cards in alphabetical order reminds you not to overlook a student.

Second-Chance Bonus Paper

Students who have no tardies or late homework for a quarter earn the right to write another paper to replace one grade during that quarter. This second chance enables students to try to raise their grade, make up an assignment, or perhaps qualify for an athletic team or scholastic achievement.
The paper must be an improvement on the previous grade, clearly written and grammatically accurate to cancel the lower grade.

Unexpected Reward

Number students on your seating charts. Make enough tokens for each student in your class and number them. Shake the tokens inside a container. Then, unexpectedly, near the end of the class period, pull out one of the tokens.

If the student who corresponds to that number does not have his or her name on the board, a reward is given. Keep school pencils, stickers, or candies handy for these winners.

Announce the student's name only if the student qualifies.

Freebies

Early in the school year, school staff members are asked to contribute 'in-school tickets" to be given away free to deserving students nominated by their teachers.

Coaches: free admission to sporting events
Drama teacher: free tickets to plays
Music teacher: free tickets to concerts, school musicals
Art teacher: tickets for a donated student work of art
Principal: one free parking permit
Cafeteria: one free lunch

Merchants in the community may want to donate, too.

Drawings are held every week or two for those students who do not misbehave during the time period of eligibility for the drawing. Teachers notify the office of the eligible students.

The principal announces the winners over the intercom on Friday afternoon, or the names are printed in the school newspaper or written on a poster displayed near the trophy case.

The Student Council is responsible for obtaining, preparing and publicizing the tickets.

Positive News Release

At the close of each semester, send out a news release to the local newspaper and radio and TV stations listing those students who have exhibited outstanding behavior in all classes and throughout the school. These students may not always be tops academically, but are known for their attitude and positive behavior.

Students need to know in advance the criteria for making this important list. Teachers should have class rules posted. Administrators should announce and post rules for schoolwide behavior.

The list is posted and also read to the student body at an assembly.

Morning Times

LOCAL STUDENTS HONORED

Two hundred students at _____ have earned a spot on the Positive Behavior Scroll for the fall semester. These students were honored because they had no tardies, no late homework, no unexcused absences from any class, and no school citations for inappropriate behavior for the entire semester.

Principal _____ issues the listing each semester to honor students who have a positive attitude toward school.

Freshmen:

Sophomores:

Juniors:

Seniors:

V.I.P. Dining Table

Establish a special table in the faculty dining area or in the principal's lounge for V.I.P. students. The student may earn a seat at this table for one day by having no tardies or no late homework for a quarter or a semester. Or you may choose other ways to earn this special seating.

Invite interesting people from the community, such as the local newspaper editor, the radio station manager, or the record store owner, to come and have lunch with the V.I.P. students. Discussions about their businesses will enlarge the horizons of the students.

Students who earn the V.I.P. privilege may also choose to bring a date.

Look Under Your Seat!

Before class, the teacher sticks a coupon in a hidden place under the seats of three students. The teacher may choose students who need to improve their behavior as well as well-behaved students.

The teacher announces that "today is Surprise Coupon Day." The students look under their seats. The three who have the coupons are in the running to qualify for a special reward to be given at the end of the period. But they must achieve the behavior goals established for the reward (completing the assignment, no talking out, etc.).

The reward can be leaving a minute early, or a positive phone call or note to the parents.

Mascot Eyes

Posters in the school remind students that the staff is watching to catch them doing something good. If the school mascot is a tiger, the poster would read: "Great Tiger Eyes Are Watching You."

As adults see students behaving appropriately or in an exemplary way, they write anonymous notes (signed "Tiger Eyes," for example) which are delivered by the principal to the students in class on Fridays.

Although these notes are a very positive boost in themselves, some schools use them as entries in a drawing or make them redeemable at the student store.

No Homework Days

This positive idea encourages students to behave appropriately in all classes on their schedule. Students work to earn no homework Fridays (or another day of the teacher's choosing) for one month. Here's what to do:

Every Thursday for a month each student receives a $3'' \times 5''$ index card listing the contest rules and a column of eight numbers.

	Period
Name_____	1
Homeroom_____	2
Rules	3
• Submit card to each teacher on Thursday.	4
• If you have behaved appropriately (no consequences) all week, the teacher will punch the number corresponding to the class period.	5
	6
	7
• A fully-punched card entitles you to skip homework on Friday.	8

In each class (including homeroom), the student submits the card to the teacher. If the student has behaved appropriately in class all week, the teacher punches the number that corresponds to the class period. Every student who returns a fully-punched card earns the privilege of skipping all homework assignments for Friday.

Students who receive four fully-punched cards for the month also earn the right to skip homework for one day of their choosing during the following month.

Thanks to Robert Fawcett of Pasadena, Texas, for this idea.

Privilege Pass

Students who achieve all the behavior goals established by their teachers and the school for a semester earn a Privilege Pass. The select group of students holding a Privilege Pass is permitted to move around campus more freely.

The pass, signed by the principal, allows them, for example, to enter the library at any time, gain extra computer time or additional athletic practice time, or be given a special parking space.

Privilege Pass holders may also have their pictures posted so that all staff and students may know who they are.

A Record of Positives

For students who always seem to misbehave, the principal and teachers can work together as a team to improve the students' behavior with a Positive Behavior Contract.

The student is called to the principal's office and receives a card marked off for each class period. The student takes the card to each class and asks each teacher to sign it if the student has met the teacher's behavior goals that period.

At the end of the day, the student brings the card back to the principal for an individual reward (such as a free movie pass or pizza dinner donated by local merchants) if all spaces are signed. If not, this is an opportunity to discuss the classes that went well and how to improve behavior in other classes. The discussion always ends with a positive comment, such as: "You did well in three classes. Let's try to make it all five tomorrow!"

Some students need to take small steps in improving their behavior. Blocking out the day into these individual steps helps them to gain control over their behavior one hour at a time.

Also, by seeing the card, teachers have the benefit of working together to help one particular student improve.

POSITIVE BEHAVIOR CONTRACT

Period   Student's Name _____

1 _____

2 _____

3 _____

4 _____

5 _____

6 _____

Adopt-A-Kid

The school counselors compile a list of probationary students (those with multiple failures and discipline problems). This list is given to all teachers, administrators, custodians, and cafeteria workers. On a voluntary basis, an adult can "adopt" one or more students and the counselor is notified. If you choose to adopt a student, here's what to do.

Call the student in for a conference. Explain that you have adopted the student so you can work together to help improve the student's grades and behavior problems. Also explain the program to the student's parents.

Every week, request that the student carry a grade check or progress report to each class and bring it to you at the end of the day. Together you talk over the problems and try to work out solutions. If the report is favorable, the student receives a reward. A free pass to a school sporting event or a school dance may be a good motivator.

You may, as the adoptive school parent, buy lunch if the student forgets lunch money, or attend ball games or plays with your adoptee.

This program works so well that other students may come in to the counseling office to ask why they were not adopted!

Thanks to Alcyone Bass, Hamilton Junior High School, Long Beach, California, for this idea.

Positive Reinforcement for the Entire Class

Positive peer pressure works wonders in a classroom. The class will work together to achieve a common reward, such as a special movie (that may also have an academic purpose). They'll urge each other not to be tardy and remind each other to turn in homework.

How to Keep Track of Positives for the Entire Class

Secondary teachers need simple methods to keep track of the points accumulating toward a class reward. Here are some useful approaches:

- Use a corner of the chalkboard, labeled Bonus Point Corner.
- Use posters created by the students or by the art class (for extra bonus points in that class).
- Use copies of your seating charts.
- Use strips of paper posted on your bulletin board for quick check-off.
- Use a clipboard.
- Select pages in your gradebook.
- Use the *Assertive Discipline Plan Book Plus*.
- Use 3″ × 5″ file cards, in a file box or an expanding folder.

Rewards for the Entire Class

On the next page is a listing of positive rewards that you can use to assist you in motivating the entire class. Some teachers enjoy asking the class to develop a list of class rewards. A little time and imagination will allow you to create your own ideas, too. Remember, choose only rewards that you feel comfortable with.

- Ice cream feed
- Movie of theater quality (appropriate to course subject)
- Special assembly for classes that meet the behavior goals
- Select-A-Seat Day
- No homework night
- Bonus points towards a grade
- Raffle for donated prizes from merchants (see sample letter on p. 39)
- Radio on during independent seat work (class may choose the station; teacher chooses the volume)
- Use the "buddy system" to work on an assignment in class
- Free reading period
- Soft drink party
- Three minutes of "primp time" at the end of class

Bonus Point Corner

A simple way to record positives is to chalk a tally mark on the board space titled Bonus Point Corner. The class works toward a reward they especially like through individual participation and group adherence to the list of rules.

When all students arrive on time to class, for example, put a tally mark in the class corner. To use peer pressure with a difficult student, say, "If Dan brings his completed homework tomorrow, I will give this class three bonus points." Prearrange with the class that if they earn 50 points within one week, for instance, they will receive an ice cream treat on Friday, or bonus points towards improving a grade.

Many teachers use class discussion to determine the kinds of rewards to establish. The teacher adapts the ideas to the classroom setting. Many students enjoy playing scholastic games or reading the sports pages. These are the kinds of rewards that enhance thinking and reading skills and though the students consider them "rewards," they are still on-task.

Coupon Mania

Prepare a box and fill it with cents-off or free coupons clipped from newspapers and magazines.

When your class meets behavior goals for a specified period of time, allow each student to draw a coupon from the box. Students may exchange coupons.

Be sure to clip favorite items of teens, such as fast food or cosmetics specials.

Winning Words

Choose a positive word for the day that is not commonly used in your students' vocabulary. Challenge your students to use this word as often as they can during the day to positively reinforce their peers' behavior.

Suggestions for positive words are: resplendent, sublime, exemplary, superlative, or phenomenal.

Make it a contest! See who can use the word appropriately most often during the day by having students record the sentence as they used it outside of class. Reward the winner or winners with free reading time or a note-writing period.

Monday Morning Quarterbacks

To encourage your sports-minded students to meet behavior goals, use posters of a football field, baseball diamond, dart board, or bowling lane. Students can help create the posters.

As students meet your behavior goals, accumulate their points by:

- advancing yardage on the football field with paper players
- drawing in another bull's-eye on the dart board
- moving a baseball player to another base around the diamond
- knocking over a bowling pin in the lane

On Monday morning following a week when behavior goals are met, the students get to read the sports pages and discuss the weekend games.

Especially for English or reading classes:
Reinforce reading skills by using the sports vocabulary as part of the weekly spelling quiz. The reward of reading the sports pages on Monday is therefore also a spelling test review.

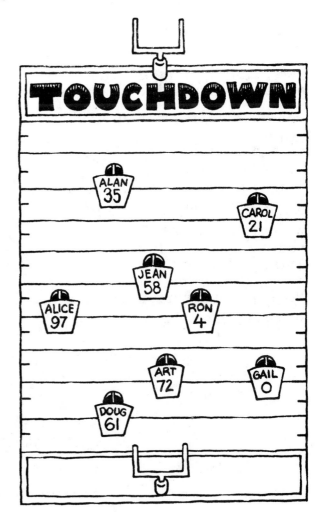

The Fortune Game

This game is not only a reward for meeting stated behavior goals, it also involves students in learning the subject matter for any course. The game is similar to the "Wheel of Fortune" television game show.

The objective of the game is to guess the letters that make up a phrase or title or object. The teacher draws blank boxes on the chalkboard that make up the chosen words of the puzzle. For example:

Divide the students into three teams. Each student on each team takes a turn and spins a cardboard spinner on a large cardboard wheel made by students as another day's reward. When the spinner stops on a space with point value, the student wins the points for the team only if he or she correctly guesses one of the consonants in the blank boxes making up the puzzle. On another turn, the team may also "buy" a vowel with points accumulated from successful spins.

For example, the student might guess the letter T. That would fill in two boxes because the words for the boxes in this puzzle are: The Old Man and the Sea. In this spin, the T is worth 1200 points. Since there are two T's, the team wins 2400 points.

At any time, one team may try to solve the puzzle. One member of the winning team gets to select the next puzzle.

Note: If the spinner lands on a space in which is a printed reminder of class rules, it has no point value and they lose a turn.

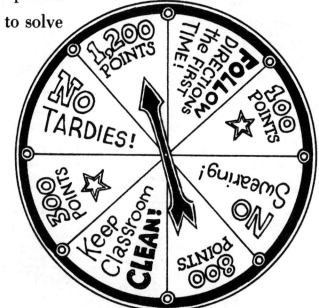

Rock Around the Clock

Each student who meets a behavior goal established by the teacher receives a round coupon shaped like a record, with "Rock Around the Clock" printed on it. The behavior goal could be that all homework assignments are completed and turned in on time for one week.

When the class as a whole has accumulated a specified number of coupons, the class members have earned any of the following rewards:

- The class may have an open discussion of 15 minutes on rock music personalities.
- Students may volunteer to speak to the class for two minutes about their favorite rock music personality.
- The class may bring in a collection of cassettes for one student to select from at random as music played during study time. (The teacher selects the volume.)

You may also use this approach to encourage individual improvements in behavior. For example, you may announce: "If Charles is not tardy tomorrow, the class earns another rock coupon toward the rock music exchange."

Thanks to Janet Foley Lakadosch of Hoffman Middle School, Aldine I.S.D., Houston, Texas, for this idea.

Big Bucks Contest

To involve students in the positive reinforcement system, ask them to design Big Bucks that will be used as rewards for meeting specified behavior goals.

Duplicate the chosen design, after a class vote, and hand out the play money for each positive behavior goal met.

Students may "spend" their Big Bucks in exchange for more computer time, library time, or listening time with a headset.

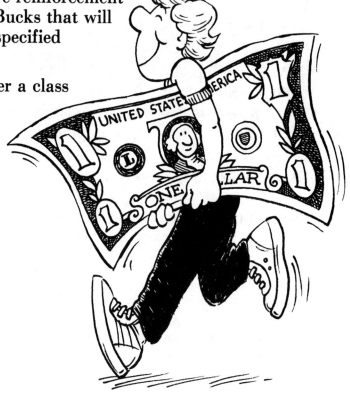

Positively News

To honor a class that has met behavior goals, take out a classified ad in the local paper or the school paper. Your ad might start out, "I would like to thank my third-period class..." and go on to list all the students' names.

Announce that your ad will soon appear, so the students will read the newspaper to find their names.

Superstar Squares

When the class has earned a reward for appropriate behavior, the game Superstar Squares is fun to play. It also helps reinforce academics.

The rules are similar to the television program "Hollywood Squares." First, select a panel of nine students who will answer a series of questions in your subject area during the game. Then select two other students as contestants, competing with each other.

To play the game, a contestant selects any one of the nine panelists to answer each question posed by the teacher. The question is multiple choice or true/false. For example: "Who warned Bostonians of the approach of the British during the Revolutionary War? Was it George Washington, Alexander Hamilton, or Paul Revere?"

The panelist chosen to answer the question may answer correctly or may choose to bluff, often humorously. But the *contestant* must judge whether the panelist's answer is correct or incorrect and state "I agree" or "I disagree."

The contestant earns points to win the game by agreeing with the correct answer or disagreeing with the incorrect answer. The teacher announces the correct answer. Rotating contestants and panelists allows everyone to play.

Some students may like being rewarded with the opportunity to write questions. All students find that playing this game helps them study for an upcoming test, reducing individual study time.

Grapevine Note Day

The Grapevine approach encourages everyone to notice positive behavior and think positively about one another.

Each student draws the name of one other student. For one week, the student records all the positives he or she observes of the other student. On Grapevine Note Day, the students give their notes to each other, after prescreening by the teacher for positives only.

Teacher Grapevine Day

The teacher announces a positive Grapevine about each student in the class.

Thanks to Debra Peppers of Lindbergh High School, St. Louis, Missouri, for this idea.

Kick-Back Friday

After four days of intensive academic work and on-target behavior, the class earns a catch-up day with the radio on (students select the station; you select the volume).

Mystery Spell-Out

This ongoing game encourages everyone in the class to support appropriate behavior throughout the class period.

To prepare, devise a question related to your subject area, for example, "Who wrote 'Gone with the Wind'?" On the board, mark chalklines that indicate each letter in this question sentence.

Then, each time you observe a student behaving in accordance with classroom rules, fill in any one of the blank chalkmarks with a letter.

As soon as there are enough letters filled in so that someone in the class can guess the answer to the question, give a classwide reward, such as three minutes of "primp" time at the end of the class.

Artists' Competition

Use graph paper pictures in art classes to help reinforce the positive behavior of individual students toward a classwide reward.

Create a picture on square-inch size graph paper for each class. It can be a picture of something seasonal for each month of the school year, such as a Halloween pumpkin, a snowflake, or a spring tulip.

Each time you wish to give positive reinforcement to an individual student, ask the student to color in one square inch of the picture. This student's behavior benefits the entire class, because the classes compete against each other for a classwide reward such as a video movie.

As the classes observe how quickly the pictures of their opponents are being colored in for positive behavior, the effort to improve behavior accelerates in each of your classes.

The first class to complete the picture wins the classwide reward and may challenge the other classes to another competition.

Variations:
- English classes may use pictures of famous authors.
- Math classes may use pictures of famous mathematicians.
- Social studies classes may use national or state maps or figures from history.
- Science classes may use pictures of famous scientists.

New Year's Tributes

Everyone likes to receive compliments. Imagine receiving an essay containing nothing but compliments about yourself! The writer is not necessarily your friend, and may even be anonymous. It's a New Year's Tribute to you.

Early in the school year, have your students draw names. Record the name drawn and the name of the student who drew it.

Throughout the semester, each student keeps a journal about the person whose name was drawn, noting all the positive accomplishments of the individual, such as talents, awards, praise given by others, assignments done well, and even compliments of a personal nature (new hairstyle, regular smile for others). Since some students can't keep a secret, the students choose whether to tell the person whose name they've drawn or to keep it a secret. It works well either way.

Approximately a week before the winter break, each student is assigned to transcribe the journal into a one- or two-page New Year's Tribute to that person — a gift of compliments and praise. No negatives are allowed (the teacher reviews and edits each tribute before it is given.)

On the day before winter break, each writer announces the recipient and reads the tribute aloud to the class. Or students may elect to receive their tributes privately to read.

Variation: All students may write a Class Tribute, contributing positive class experiences for the whole semester.

Thanks to Debra Peppers of Lindbergh High School, St. Louis, Missouri, for this idea.

Measure with Pleasure

Your classes can compete for good behavior using science measuring lessons.

Set up six tall 1000 milliliter graduated cylinders, one for each of your classes. To positively reinforce each individual and class behavior desired, drop a marble in the cylinder for that class.

The class that reaches the 1000 milliliter level first gets the Grand Positive Reinforcer; have a soft-drink party or a special select-your-own-seat day. For an alternative to measuring by milliliters, measure the marbles by mass or weight. Or use lightweight objects like poker chips and a triple beam balance to weight the jar, subtracting the weight of the jar cylinder. Determine in advance the number of grams to use to win the award.

Atomic Reinforcement

If you have a laminated Atomic Orbital Chart for your science classroom, use it to record positive reinforcement for one of your classes.

When the class is on-task, they earn electrons, filled in with colored pens on the chart. When the level-one orbital is filled, the class earns the reward specified at the side of the chart.

Each filled level earns a new reward.

Thanks to Diane Pawasarat of Salem Central High School, Salem, Wisconsin, for this idea.

Positive Reinforcement for the Entire School

How to Publicize Schoolwide Positive Reinforcement

For behavior that requires an all-school effort, such as keeping a clean campus, a series of schoolwide rewards is effective. Keep the student body motivated by constantly informing them of the goal.

- Display posters throughout the school.
- Use the trophy case — honoring positive behavior is as important as winning a sports title.
- Announce in the daily bulletin and over the intercom.
- Hang a banner across the main entrance hall.

Rewards for the Entire School

- A special assembly featuring an individual or group the students would enjoy hearing
- A picnic on the lawn, if clean-up is complete each time
- An extra after-school dance, especially during dreary days of winter
- Drawings and raffles for donated prizes from merchants (see sample letter, p. 39)
- A free performance of the school play
- A costume day in a month other than October
- Hat Day
- Singing-in-the-Halls Day
- Teacher Homeroom Treat Day (teachers bring donuts or cookies for their homeroom class)
- Cake Day (adults on the staff bring in cakes and serve slices to the students in the cafeteria)

Caught-In-The-Act Gold Slips

Staff members who "catch students being good" anywhere in the school may instantly award them a Gold Slip. Print the student's name on the Gold Slip and sign it.

Students work towards collecting a predetermined number of Gold Slips to be redeemed for a special reward, such as a free yearbook for 10 Gold Slips.

Or the student's Gold Slips may be entered in a drawing for other rewards such as stereo tapes donated by merchants, or food coupons from fast-food outlets. (See sample letter to merchants on p. 39)

GOLD SLIP

AWARDED TO

_____

TEACHER

GOLD SLIP

AWARDED TO

_____

TEACHER

GOLD SLIP

AWARDED TO

_____

TEACHER

GOLD SLIP

AWARDED TO

_____

TEACHER

GOLD SLIP

AWARDED TO

_____

TEACHER

GOLD SLIP

AWARDED TO

_____

TEACHER

The Great Escape

The principal can encourage students to employ positive peer pressure to improve each other's behavior by announcing: "If I have fewer than four referrals to my office in one week, the student body will receive 10 minutes of extended lunch, or early dismissal."

To arrive at what the number of referrals will be, use this rule of thumb: 400 students equals one referral, 800 students equals two referrals, and so forth.

Keep track of referrals on a bulletin board in the hallway or some place the entire student body can see the score. Use a weekly graph, numbered cards, or large X's cut from red construction paper to indicate the number of referrals that have taken place that week. Place the scoring system behind glass.

This technique can also be used to keep students working together towards a common schoolwide goal. For example, to ensure a clean campus, free of litter, the principal announces occasionally, "If the campus is clean at the end of the day (or by two o'clock) when I make my inspection, I will dismiss all classes 10 minutes early."

Car Giveaway

The principal gets a local car dealer to give an old car to the school. (This could be a tax write-off for the dealer.)

The car is fixed up by the industrial arts classes as a project.

Throughout the year, the students accumulate tickets for good behavior and certain academic goals (e.g., homework completed for a full month).

On the last day of school, a drawing is held on the school parking lot for the winner of the car. (Obtain parental permission for the student to accept the car.)

V.I.P. Parking Space

The principal designates one up-front parking space as the Student V.I.P. Parking Space. (In large schools two spaces may be needed.) The space is an especially coveted reward for those students who love their cars and want to show them off where everyone walks past.

Each staff member receives a few special V.I.P. Parking Space coupons. The staff member awards a student demonstrating exemplary behavior a coupon good for one day's V.I.P. Parking. The student's name is printed on the coupon with the staff member's signature below.

The student takes the coupon to the office and signs up for a day to use the V.I.P. Parking Space. This is done in advance so students who do not own cars may borrow a car, or redeem the coupon for some other preferred reward.

A large poster in the main hall announces those students who have earned the V.I.P. Parking Space.

After-School Dance

This idea helps to improve the behavior of students in targeted areas thoughout the school where problems appear to exist.

Two batches of tickets representing the school colors (for example, green and yellow) are produced. Each teacher is given 25 green tickets and instructed to distribute the tickets to students as they "catch 'em being good" in the targeted areas (yard, cafeteria). The principal is given 25 yellow tickets to give out to students who display exemplary behavior in these areas. As students receive the tickets, they deposit them in a central location.

At the end of the month, the grade level with the most green tickets is awarded an After-School Dance. The yellow tickets are turned over to the principal who draws the names of five winners and awards them special prizes, perhaps a T-shirt or pencils with the school logo.

Perfect Attendance Award

This schoolwide idea encourages good attendance. It operates on three levels: by the month, by the semester, and by the year.

Each month, the names of students who have not been absent for the entire month are placed in the "Perfect Attendance" box located in the office. On the last day of the month a name is drawn from each grade level, and the winners are awarded a cassette tape or record album of their choice.

Prizes of greater value are also awarded for perfect attendance in a semester. And, at the end of the year, one student from each grade level receives a special award for perfect attendance during the entire year — a season pass to the local amusement park!

☆ Perfect ☆	☆ Perfect ☆
MONTH _____ GRADE _____	MONTH _____ GRADE _____
ATTENDANCE	ATTENDANCE
☆ Perfect ☆	☆ Perfect ☆
MONTH _____ GRADE _____	MONTH _____ GRADE _____
ATTENDANCE	ATTENDANCE
☆ Perfect ☆	☆ Perfect ☆
MONTH _____ GRADE _____	MONTH _____ GRADE _____
ATTENDANCE	ATTENDANCE

Grade Your School

This idea utilizes peer pressure to improve the overall behavior of a school.

A committee of administrators and teachers lists 10 behaviors that need upgrading in order to improve the overall climate of the school (tardiness, inappropriate language, littering, problems on buses, excessive referrals). Every staff member, including bus drivers, custodial staff and secretaries, is given a report card and asked to grade the school on each of the 10 behaviors (A, B, C, and so forth). The point average (2.0, 2.5, 3.0) is used as a baseline. Each week thereafter the staff is given additional report cards and asked to grade the school again.

When the students improve their behavior and the point average exceeds that on the first report card, the students receive one letter of the words SUPER STUDENTS. As soon as all of the letters in the words SUPER STUDENTS are posted on the office wall or window, the entire student body is rewarded with an afternoon of special activities to choose from, such as a movie in the auditorium, a basketball game, a Trivial Pursuit contest, or a dance.

REPORT CARD					
Behavior	A	B	C	D	F
1. Tardiness	✔				
2. Truancy		✔			
3. Littering	✔				
4. Referrals			✔		
5. Bus behavior					✔
6. Inappropriate language				✔	
7. Behavior in study hall			✔		
8. Behavior in the cafeteria				✔	
9. Behavior in the halls			✔		
10. Behavior in the yard					✔

Thanks to Will Duke and Art Anderson of Banks, Oregon, for this idea.

Sample Letter to Local Merchants

Elicit the support of local merchants for your positive program by requesting free gifts and services or discounts. Send a letter explaining the Schoolwide Discipline Plan and a certificate for the merchant to fill out and return to you.

Suggested merchants are: fast food restaurants, stationery stores, computer stores, drug stores, hair salons, bicycle shops, candy stores, video stores, clothing stores, T-shirt shops, and movie theaters.

Use the certificates on the next page for soliciting merchandise.

Dear Merchant:

We at Monroe Junior High School are seeking businesses to sponsor what we feel is a unique program for our students. Very often students who conduct themselves in a mature, responsible manner are not recognized for their appropriate behavior. Instead we take their good behavior for granted and focus on the students who misbehave. In an effort to balance the attention given to students, we have developed a plan at Monroe Junior High School that provides negative consequences for those who violate the school rules and at the same time provides positive reinforcement for those who act as mature young citizens.

As a part of the positive reinforcement component of our behavior management plan, we intend to distribute Gold Slips as a reward for good behavior. These slips will be used in a schoolwide drawing to give away prizes. That is why we are writing to you to ask if you would like to participate by donating prizes for our drawing.

We feel that you, as a merchant in our area, can benefit from participating in our program. You will be promoting good behavior which can carry over when students leave the school and enter your place of business. We also feel that parents accompanying children who pick up prizes may buy something while there. In addition, you will receive free publicity by being recognized as one of our sponsors and as a merchant who cares about the young people of our community.

If you are interested in participating in our program, we will gladly accept any assistance you can offer.

Sincerely,

Principal

MERCHANT CERTIFICATE

_____
Name of Merchant or Business

is proud to be part of the Assertive Discipline program. We believe that students who act as mature, responsible citizens should be recognized. Therefore, if the student named below will present this certificate at:

_____
Address of Business

on or before the date of _____ , this
student will receive _____ .
Description of Gift

The winner must be accompanied by a parent or guardian and must present his or her school ID card along with this certificate in order to receive the gift.

_____   _____
Merchant's signature   *Student's name*

_____   _____
Date issued   *Principal's signature*

MERCHANT CERTIFICATE

_____
Name of Merchant or Business

is proud to be part of the Assertive Discipline program. We believe that students who act as mature, responsible citizens should be recognized. Therefore, if the student named below will present this certificate at:

_____
Address of Business

on or before the date of _____ , this
student will receive _____ .
Description of Gift

The winner must be accompanied by a parent or guardian and must present his or her school ID card along with this certificate in order to receive the gift.

_____   _____
Merchant's signature   *Student's name*

_____   _____
Date issued   *Principal's signature*